DINO TIME LINE

by Carl Escobedo
Illustrated by Gary Torrisi

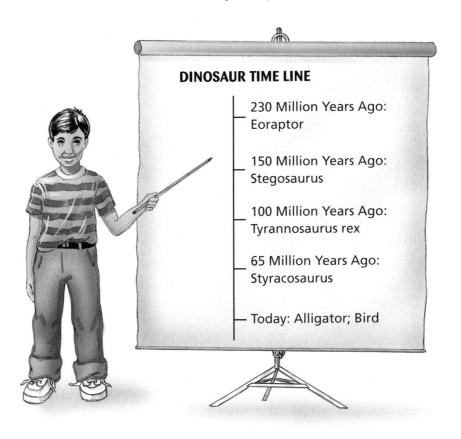

DINOSAUR TIME LINE

230 Million Years Ago:
Eoraptor

150 Million Years Ago:
Stegosaurus

100 Million Years Ago:
Tyrannosaurus rex

65 Million Years Ago:
Styracosaurus

Today: Alligator; Bird

PEARSON

Glenview, Illinois • Boston, Massachusetts • Chandler, Arizona
Upper Saddle River, New Jersey

dinosaur

LONG, LONG AGO

The poem on these pages is not about now.
It's not about a dog, or a cat, or a cow.
This poem is about dinosaurs long, long ago,
Who died in the past—in the heat or the snow.

Did You Know? **Alligators**

Alligators live in our world today. Like dinosaurs, they are cold-blooded. Some alligators are 15 feet long. Alligators are reptiles. Dinosaurs were too.

---

cold-blooded: not able to warm or cool their bodies unless the air around them is warm or cool

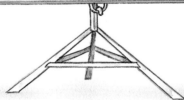

Paleontologists are scientists who study dinosaurs. They know that **Eoraptor** (EE oh RAP tor) and **Saltopus** (SAL to pus) lived about 230 million years ago. Paleontologists don't know a lot about Saltopus. They are not even sure that Saltopus was a dinosaur.

230 MILLION YEARS AGO

Now the fast **Eoraptor**—it was quite small.
But it might have been the first dinosaur of all.
Saltopus—it was still smaller than that.
it was the size of a friendly house cat.

---

paleontologists: scientists who study prehistoric life, or life long before people had writing

plates

spikes

plants

Stegosaurus (steg o SAW rus) Its small teeth were not good for protection, or keeping it safe. But its plates and spikes probably were good protection. Some scientists think its plates helped to cool its body too.

150 MILLION YEARS AGO

A long time later, **Stegosaurus** was around.
With big plates down its back, it was heavy on the ground.
The spikes on its tail helped it fight in a battle.
But it ate only plants, just like today's cattle.

---

cattle: cows and bulls

allosaurus

diplodocus

Many dinosaurs were very large. **Allosaurus** (AL leh SORE rus) was 38 feet long! It walked on two legs. Allosaurus was a meat-eater. It chased, killed, and ate other dinosaurs, including **Diplodocus** (di PLOD eh kus). Diplodocus was a 90-foot long plant-eater.

Allosaurus was around at the same time, or just a bit later,
Still many long years before our alligator.
This beast was huge, with big, sharp teeth.
Unlike Stegosaurus, it ate dinosaur meat!

---

beast: animal or creature

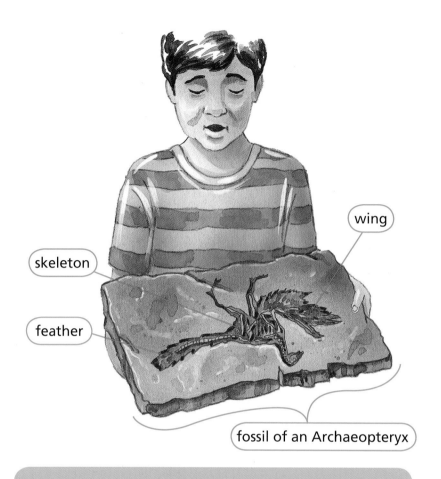

skeleton

wing

feather

fossil of an Archaeopteryx

Archaeopteryx (ar kay OP tur iks) had wings and feathers. Some scientists say it was an early bird, not a dinosaur. Maybe it could fly; maybe it could not. Scientists are not sure.

Now you might imagine some dinosaurs in the sky—
Archaeopteryx, for one—but I doubt it could fly.
With feathers and wings, it was almost a bird
But didn't have the right bones for flying, I've heard.

Tyrannosaurus rex (tih ran uh SAWR uhs REX) was a fierce meat-eater. **Styracosaurus** (sty RACK oh SORE us) was a plant-eater, but had dangerous spikes or horns. On some occasions, Styracosaurus could win a fight against Tyrannosaurus.

100 MILLION YEARS AGO

The fiercest of all dinosaurs came along later.
Its teeth remind me of an alligator's.
This killing machine was called **Tyrannosaurus**.
You wouldn't want to meet one in a dark forest!
But **Styracosaurus** wouldn't give me a scare.
Sure she had spikes, for defense, but that's fair.
Tyrannosaurus was hungry; he wanted to eat her.
But the horns on her head could defeat the meat-eater.

---

fierce: violent and powerful

DINOSAUR TIME LINE

- 230 Million Years Ago: Eoraptor
- 150 Million Years Ago: Stegosaurus
- 100 Million Years Ago: Tyrannosaurus rex
- 65 Million Years Ago: Styracosaurus
- Today: Alligator; Bird

65 MILLION YEARS AGO

Some paleontologists say long ago in the past
The dinosaurs died from a great volcano blast.
Others think that an asteroid from space
Hit the earth and made it a very hot place.
Some scientists think it was cold, not the heat,
That killed off these creatures we never can meet.
Whatever happened, it changed the Earth's weather,
And dinosaurs died off forever and ever

---

volcano: mountain that sends hot rocks, ash, and gas into the sky
asteroid: very large rock that moves through space